AF290490

"Gutten Abend" (good evening) were the first words that two Soviet soldiers addressed in German to the frightened population when they marched into Knoblauch, a small village near Berlin. They were these words which took away the pent-up fear of the people intimidated by the propaganda and coverage of the terrible events of the war.

Personal experiences during the time between the end of the war and the immediate post-war period in and around Berlin of a boy and his mother who had previously fled West Prussia and who had experienced the heavy bombing raids in the last phase of the Second World War show a partly different picture than that, whatever has always been presented as historical facts.

Herstellung und Verlag:
BoD - Books on Demand, Norderstedt
ISBN 978-3-7534-0152-2

THAT WAS ALSO THE INVASION OF THE RUSSIAN ARMY IN GERMANY

Memories of

Lothar Hans Schreiber

As far as the text refers to **WIKIPEDIA**, a more detailed explanation can be found under the main keyword

My mother and I had gone to West Prussia south of Danzig because of the increasing bombing raids on Berlin, where my mother's parents lived and my mother worked as a teacher. In the first days of January 1945 we had to flee. To be precise, soldiers of the Wehrmacht were quartered in my mother's school in the Briesen district, who had to leave shortly afterwards and took my mother and me with them. My mother didn't think the danger was that great yet, but the soldiers talked until we went along with the entourage. We were taken to Graudenz and put on a train full of refugees, although we were lucky and only needed three days to get to Küstrin on the Oder. We stayed there for two days with my paternal grandmother, and then went to the nearby Sonnenburg, where my parents owned a house that they had rented. Our tenant made one room available for us. But after about three more days we were woken up in the morning by our tenant's daughter with the information that the Russians were approaching and the last train from Sonnenburg to Küstrin would leave in an hour.

We got dressed as quickly as we could and hurried to the train station. We managed to get to Küstrin old town with the last train. When we arrived at my grandmother's, my father's mother, my aunt welcomed us with the words: "If you still want to go to Berlin, then you have to hurry because the last train leaves in two hours." We wanted to go to Berlin because we still had our apartment there. Shortly before the end of the war, it was placed on hold. When we arrived in Berlin, we first looked for our aunt Paula near the Friedrichhain because there was a bunker very close to it. The first night we wanted to stay in Berlin again was supposed to be near the large bunker that protected it. There was also an air raid promptly. We felt safe in the bunker there. But the next day We wanted to go to our apartment on Gitschiner Strasse. Before we went to them, we went briefly to Fraulein Neumann's cellar store to buy some groceries when the air raid alarm came. It was February 3, 1945. We walked into the public shelter of the patent office, a very long, narrow corridor reinforced with concrete in Gitschiner Strasse. It was the first really big attack on Berlin with very heavy destruction of about 80% of the inner city and many dead. According to American estimates, there were around 22,000 to 25,000 fatalities (Plotz, Extract from History 1986, p. 909). I described what we experienced there in the newspaper "Die Welt" on February 3, 2000. The editorial team mistakably stated that the rooms were at ground level and around 200 meters deep.

The depth was not meant vertical but horizontal. After the air raid was over, the patent office was partially hit, but we got out of the shelter alive, it was impossible to walk east along Gitschiner Strasse because the flames hissed over from the right and formed a barrier wall. There was a very strong firestorm.

As I already described at the time, we stumbled almost headless in fear because we feared another air raid, because the air raid warden had pointed out when leaving the shelters that another immediate bombing was to be expected. So we stumbled on the other side of the Landwehr Canal. My mother had panic. She just wanted to get away.

We walked along Blücherstrasse to today's Südstern and were picked up in Hasenheide by a truck that took us to the next functional S-Bahn station. The damage was much less on the southern side of the Landwehr Canal. We took the S-Bahn to Königs-Wusterhausen, south-east of Berlin. There we were housed with many other people in the large broadcasting hall of the German broadcaster. My mother really wanted to stay in the country West of Berlin. So we drove on to Nauen, about 40 km from Berlin, because we were still officially refugees from West Prussia, and from there we were sent to Etzin, a village, and then forwarded to Knoblauch to another village. Knoblauch was near Ketzin an der Havel, a small town in the Mark Brandenburg region.

According to WIKIPEDIA, Knoblauch was an over 800 years old village that was abandoned in 1968/69 because of the construction of a natural gas storage facility. It's completely gone. Knoblauch is a place full of memories only for us, even if it no longer exists. We stayed with the K. family, a farming family without male farmers (for reasons of data protection, the name cannot be given, but is contained in the book "Ketzin 1945", ERS-Verlag 1996). It consisted of two sisters, the old suffering mother, a grandson, the son-in-law and a Polish prisoner of war Ludwig, who ran the business as far as a man was necessary. Ludwig disappeared immediately with the invasion of the Soviet troops. It wasn't until much later that we heard that our apartment in Berlin belonged to a house which had remained standing along with 8 other houses on Gitschiner Strasse. In any case, we stayed in

Knoblauch until after the invasion of the Soviet Army. It is my intention to describe this and the following time.

There was only one old teacher working in Knoblauch. When he heard that my mother, Frieda Schreiber, had worked as a teacher in West Prussia until December 1944, he persuaded her to try again to become a teacher in Nauen and to teach in Knoblauch. It also worked. The mayor and some large farmers had fled to the west in horse-drawn vehicles in the past few days. The front had slowly moved closer to Berlin and the propaganda never missed an opportunity to report on the atrocities of the Russians in the east of the country. We expected the "end of the world".

The teacher was called up for the Volkssturm. There were only a number of Knoblauch residents left. Somehow it happened that my mother was the only official person to take over the management of the village for a short time, quite unbureaucratically and informally. This is also evident from "Ketzin

1945", page 48, by Bergemann and Damaschke.

You have to remember that for all of us in Knoblauch, fear was our constant companion. Every day the Allied planes flew with their bomb load over us to Berlin. When they flew back they mostly dropped one or more bombs on the rural area where we now lived. The air raid on Dresden and its large number of deaths, which could not be quantified precisely because of the unknown number of refugees from the east who passed through and found no protection, even later. We also became aware of this attack. It increased our fears, our worries and almost led to panic reactions. In addition, there were the daily radio broadcasts about inhumane acts of the Soviet soldiers against us Germans, especially women.

The air raid on Potsdam on the late evening of April 14, 1945, during which we saw the eerily beautiful bright sky over Potsdam in Knoblauch and heard the doors in their locks rattle because of the air pressure - the sound of the exploding bombs was no longer so loud in Knoblauch - but everything together increased our fear, especially since the number of about 1,600 deaths became known very quickly.

According to WIKIPEDIA, it was probably April 21, 1945. My mother, I and a few older people stood in the village square, tormented again and again by fear and worry because of all these events. My mother wanted to hang a white flag on the church tower when two young maybe 16—year-old girls came running up screaming. They shouted, (or rather they shouted: "They are coming, they are coming", when we asked who is coming, they replied: "Well, the Russians, the Russians!" And in fact two Soviet soldiers on bicycles came slowly approaching us, in each hand a pistol. A long column of Russian soldiers marched behind them, their rifles or their typical Russian submachine guns with their characteristic drum magazines slung around their necks. There were maybe 150 soldiers.

We held our breath with the anxious question in our hearts, what will happen when the cyclists stopped, came up to us and said:

"Gutten Abend (good evening) woyna kaputt, Gittler tott" (war broken, Hitler dead). Both Soviet soldiers spoke more than a few words of German and also said we needn't be afraid. We didn't expect that, it made us almost speechless. However, it had a very calming effect and slowly resolved our anxious tensions, especially since the German radio station had always emphasized the Russian atrocities up until then.

The column of soldiers also stopped and scowled at us. As we were standing in the village square opposite to the grocery store of the merchant E. K...w (name not mentioned due to data protection) also selling tobacco and alcoholic beverages, we saw that some Russian soldiers from the back rows with rifle butts or something similar banged the door and, above all, took out tobacco and schnapps. Some German villagers followed, who also showed up now. They also went to the store. An uncle of my mother, an old man from Berlin who had been afraid of the final battles in Berlin, had joined us. This uncle also went to the shop entrance, but not into the shop itself.

However, he said to a Soviet soldier who came out with an armful of packets of tobacco: "Give me tobacco too, brad". The Russian replied "Nix brad", but gave him a small packet of tobacco. It is perhaps interesting to know that despite all the cries for victory in the last few months before the end of the war, small Russian language gauges and phrasebooks had been sold, so that the word brad, namely brother, was well known. All this was a situation we hadn't imagined.

In any case, the grocery store was broken into by Soviet soldiers from the bottom ranks of the column and not, as the WIKIPEDIA report on the village of Knoblauch says, by Germans. I was standing close by and watching everything. Various Germans went into the shop behind the Russians and helped each other. After a while, when in our opinion everything remained relatively calm, we went to sleep fairly relaxed. The next day the great crowd of soldiers was gone; apparently only a few remained. It was said later that around two to three young women were raped that night. The next day the foreign workers left the farmers in

Knoblauch, where they had to work, and took some clothes and valuables with them. I also remember that they wanted to take two cars with them. One was a Mercedes that couldn't start and the other was a DKW that didn't work. The DKW had stopped in the middle of the village. We children and teenagers enjoyed ourselves by pushing the car up a very small hill, then jumping in and driving down that small hill. It was all peaceful. Both cars were cannibalized over the next few days. Then, however, men and women and young people aged 14 and over were asked by the

Russian military in Knoblauch to come to the village with spades and shovels in order to provisionally create an airfield, that is an airfield south of the village. My mother also had to take part. As far as I can remember, they all worked for 2 to 3 days with no particular incident. Soon the airfield was built according to the ideas of the Soviet soldiers. Biplanes also landed a few times, probably of the U-2 type. But that was over very quickly.

Time went on, as far as I remember, we only had two Soviet soldiers as a crew in the days that followed, at least that is how it seemed to me. We could buy bread from the village baker again. It was probably on May 4th, 1945, according to Henrik Schulze, "19 Days of War", 2011, page 337, it was May 2nd when German soldiers coming from Berlin wanted to make their way west. From my point of view at the time, it was they who started fighting again and shot into the village. Knoblauch was not so badly damaged in these battles in contrast to Etzin, the neighboring village, which showed considerable damage. The stable of the K. farm, where we lived, was hit by a grenade. The farmers and we were in a cellar in the barn. The owner's son-in—law, M., was standing on the threshing floor of the barn when the grenade struck the stable and splinters injured him. He died of the wounds several weeks later. He was probably the only civilian who died as a result of this fight. Knoblauch had been ingested again by the German military. When suddenly it was said that the fight would be intensified again after 6 pm if the German troops did not surrender. My mother and I were so horrified that we decided to leave the village of Knoblauch as quickly as possible

and go towards the Russian front
The fact that two adolescents were
delighted that we would be German
again because of the renewed
presence of German Wehrmacht
soldiers and threatened my mother
because she had intended to raise
the white flag, strengthened our
decision.

We walked and stumbled together
with our old uncle in the direction
of Paretz, a neighboring community,
while we crossed an area in which
Soviet soldiers had armed
themselves to fight. There were
probably some injuries and deaths

in this area. We didn't see anyone exactly because we hurried on, we were very scared. The Soviet soldiers gestured towards Paretz and pointed to the area behind them. One of the Russian soldiers said "Woyna, woyna" (war, war) and was able to point out that at around 6:00 am (6:00 pm) the fight would certainly start again and we should leave as soon as possible.

We reached Paretz and had to pass two fallen Soviet soldiers to get into the village. There was no one on the street. When we were suddenly approached by an older man from a rather representative house and asked where we were going. Because we didn't know, he invited us into his house and we could take a seat with his family in his rather large basement and spend the night. We did not understand why he invited us. When the next day the battle had still not started, we left the house and went back to Knoblauch. We assumed there would be no more battle, which we were right about. The two dead Russians were gone, and the battlefield had also disbanded. Various weapons were still lying around. We were asked about our documents about twice by Soviet soldiers and a civilian each. We couldn't find out whether they could read it, but we were allowed to continue towards Knoblauch, but now with less fear. We did not see any dead or injured. Corresponding assertions in H. Schulze, page 359, we could in no way confirm with regard to the way back. The Russian soldiers in combat positions were gone. The Knoblauch windmill had been set on fire. This mill was characteristic in that, as far as I can remember, it only had 2 blades.

When we arrived at our farmer's house, we found that our room was occupied by a Russian sergeant, as we later discovered. There were also two other soldiers in the house. My mother and I slept in the attic. The next day I was playing on the village square in hem of the farmhouse and found a saber that I liked and that I took with me into the yard when the Russian sergeant saw me. He took the saber from me with the words " nix gudd,Kinder" (not good, children), tried to bend the saber and threw it into the cesspool there. But he gave me a whip for it, a nine-tailed cat. After two more days, the soldiers left the farm. The sergeant had only used my smaller bed.

A few days passed again when it was said that there was a large Wehrmacht food depot in Ketzin. The Soviets would distribute boxes of sardines there. Although we, my mother and my great-uncle couldn't believe it, we made our way to Ketzin, about three kilometers. I had found an old lady's bike frame and also rims with spokes on the street that I screwed together with primitive screws. You could push this "bike" without tires, but with a luggage rack. All sorts of things could be found on the street in Knoblauch. We actually got to this depot and, oh wonder, all in all, my mother and I received three boxes filled with a hundred cans of Portuguese sardines each. The depot was probably only emptied after two more days.

We never knew why the Russians gave this food away. Was it good-naturedness or did they think the sardines were poisoned? The sardines helped us, my mother, me and later my father to survive the greatest starvation period for three years. We used it very sparingly. In their report "'Ketzin 1945" page 19, Bergemann and Damaschke mention these sardines, which not only the Ketzins received, but also people like us from distant villages. Word quickly got around about the distribution of sardines to the German population. We were not aware of the considerable acts of sexual violence against women in Ketzin (page 15) mentioned by Bergemann and Damaschke. At that time, it was possible that Knoblauch was assumed not to exist or that it was not so big.

In general, the opinion prevailed in some places west from Berlin to the river Elbe that women were raped in these areas far less or hardly at all. In any case, in Saarland after reunification, I came across speakers item the western GDR who reported on the peacefulness of Russian soldiers in various lectures.

Violent excesses by soldiers of the Russian army against German women in general, on the other hand, have been described by many historians and contemporary witnesses, including Soviet ofiicers such as Lev Kopelew and

Alexander Solschenizin, on the triumphal march from the Reich border to the final battle in Berlin. The thirst for revenge was just very great. The misdeeds on the German side were also very great. For Hitler the war was a worldview and race war, so he called for the extermination of the Russian people, Russians were for him an inferior race. In the exhibition "The Soviet Paradise" in Berlin in 1942, life in the Soviet Union was portrayed as extremely primitive. With this exhibition, German propaganda probably wanted to justify the attack on Russia by showing a completely falsified and degrading image of Russia at that time, according to WIKIPEDIA. I had visited this exhibition when I was eight years old with an uncle; because my mother and I had come to Berlin from West Prussia at short notice at this time.

The historical accounts also speak of individual cases in which Russian soldiers and army doctors were very generous. It is worth mentioning that a military hospital was set up in Paretz near Ketzin, in which both German and Russian injured persons were treated by

German and Russian nursing staff and German doctors (Bergemann and Damaschke, page 27). With this I want to point out that the experiences of my mother, the short-term teacher in Knoblauch and me were by no means that extraordinary.

Soon after that we made our way to Berlin. We didn't know whether our apartment on Gitschiner Strasse was still there. It was said that freight trains with booty from the Soviet Army would stop in Röthehof and that people could be taken as far as Berlin. My mother and I, we joined a small group of people who made our way to Röthehof. On a street near Vorketzin, two courageous older men stopped a Soviet military truck and asked the soldiers if they would let us go with them, and this vehicle really took us all as far as Röthehof. The Russian soldiers helped the two women to climb onto the truck without any fights. So there was, oh wonder, no trouble with the Soviet soldiers. We walked the last stretch to the station stop in Röthehof and at some point a freight train came - all flat freight cars - loaded with dismantled railroad tracks, which stopped and took us and others with it. It actually stopped at the partly destroyed Schlesischer Bahnhof (today Ost-Bahnhof). We could get down.

My mother and I walked to our apartment through very badly damaged Berlin. Hardly believable, we found our apartment on Gitschiner Strasse. It still existed. But it was occupied. The houses from Brandenburgstrasse, today Lobeckstrasse, to Alexandrinenstrasse stood in Gitschiner Strasse. Other parts of Gitschiner Strasse, Prinzenstrasse and the areas above Moritzplatz and far beyond, such as the entire center, were badly damaged or completely destroyed by the air raid on February 3, 1945.

It was agreed with the residents of our apartment that they would release it as soon as they found a place to stay that they actually found soon. In any case, we went to see my mother's aunt on Heinrich-Roller-Strasse north of the Königstor. As far as I can remember, there were also double-decker buses running on some lines. In any case, we stayed with the aunt for two days and then made our way back to Knoblauch. We walked to Knie, a square in Charlottenburg, which is now called Ernst-Reuter-Platz, and could take the subway from Knie to Ruhleben. It was the first underground line in Berlin to be restored after the end of the war. It was the short-term city commandant General Bersarin who tried to bring about a quick order, but who very soon fell victim to a traffic accident and died. It has probably not been clarified whether he was killed because he was considered too friendly to Germany.

From Ruhleben we set out on foot via Spandau, Wustermark to Knoblauch, about 45 km. Signs, that had already been put up, were remarkable with inscriptions such as "The Hitler come and go, but the German people remain, JW Stalin". Stalin had already uttered this saying in 1942 (NM Naimark, Die Russen in Deutschland, page 100), in the following years of war, however, no longer used, but considered appropriate again in 1945. We passed a barracks in Döberitz occupied with Russian soldiers. A soldier spoke to us, asked "sick" and let us go on or rather stagger because we were very tired. In the evening we arrived in Knoblauch.

Soon afterwards we drove from Wustermark to the Silesian station (Schlesischer Bahnhof) in Berlin with a freight train to which passenger cars were already attached. In the compartment sat a Russian soldier who spoke broken German. He was a prisoner of war in Germany, he said, and is now part of the Red Army again. We don't know how far this is true. In fact, the train stopped at

Schlesischer Bahnhof and we were able to get off.

We were able to move back into our apartment on Gitschiner Strasse after living in the small apartment with the allocated tenants for a few days. These other tenants found other accommodation and moved out. We lived more poorly than well for the next few weeks, but we lived. An epidemic of diphtheria occurred in Berlin, partly in connection with scarlet fever, and my mother immediately fell ill with it. Amazingly, I did not get infected. I took her to a makeshift hospital on

Bergmannstrasse, from where she was soon transferred to the largely intact Urban hospital and survived.

After I had brought her to Bergmannstrasse, I took the subway from Gardepionierplatz - today Südstern - as far as I could go north, probably to Alexanderplatz - and walked crying loudly because I felt so alone when I passed the square at the Königstor, to Heinrich-Roller-Strasse, where I knew my aunt lived. From Alexanderplatz to Königstor, all or almost all buildings were completely destroyed or badly damaged. From Königstor to the north, meaning Greifswalder Strasse and the area of Prenzlauer Berg district in general, were considerably less bombed or war-damaged.

Although very sad about my mother's illness, I made friends with my aunt's a little older boy. He told me that in a primitively furnished shop in the ruins of the Hertie building on Alexanderplatz there would be razors with ten blades in a Bakelite case for 4.50 Reichsmarks. You could use them for barter deals. In fact, I was able to buy such a razor with blades.

Soon after, my new friend recommended that I take him to Weissensee. Russian trucks with soldiers would stop there in hunt of a restaurant on the Weissensee. It is interesting to stay there briefly. Since the tram was already driving along Greifswalder Strasse from Königstor to Weissensee, I got up and drove there. I took my razor blades and razor with me thinking, you never know. At Weissensee there were actually a large number of Soviet trucks of American origin in front of a pub - probably only open to the Russian military. These were characterized by the fact that they had no doors, but rather a kind of oval entry below. In front of such a truck I saw a 14 to 15-year-old boy who looked into the driver's cab of such a truck and was obviously rummaging around in it. Although Russian soldiers chased him away several times, he kept going. Then one of the soldiers, who appeared to be a sergeant, pulled out his pistol and obviously pointed it at the boy. We children standing around believed that the soldier would shoot this boy. But the soldier just shot in the air. The result, however, was that the boy stumbled away.

I stayed there for a while and continued to watch the scene with great interest. When again, as often an open car with Russian officers arrived, it was a German "Horch", which was obviously very popular with the officers, and stopped, I took my heart and walked towards the car. I held out my Bakelite box with the razor and razor blades to the soldiers. Indeed, one of the officers took my box, opened it, and removed the razor blades. He handed the rest back to me. Then he reached into his wallet, took 50 Allied marks and gave them to me. It must be noted that at the time the Allies had issued their own currency that was worth more than our Reichsmarks. Amazed and delighted, I accepted the money and almost immediately drove back to my aunt on Heirnich-Roller-Strasse.

A few days later I was walking along Greifswalder Strasse, not very far from the Märchenbrunnen in Friedrichshain, when a Russian truck stopped in front of me, laden with a white mass. A Soviet soldier sitting in the back called me and asked me to give him my cap. Although it was warm, I wore a ski cap. I gave it to him and he filled it with the white mass. It was sugar, about a pound and a half. Several people came up to the vehicle after me and were delighted to receive sugar. I took the sugar back to my aunt. I had a similar experience a few days later in Prenzlauer Allee.

My mother soon recovered and I was able to return to our apartment with her. We lived right and wrong as the post-war conditions allowed. Around May 1946, a boy friend from my street told me that the Soviet Army had set up summer camps around Berlin where girls and boys up to the age of 21 could spend 14 days of school vacation for 20 Reichsmarks and without food stamps. Young people from all over Berlin, both from East and West Berlin, were allowed to take part. The office where you could apply was on the corner of Kronenstrasse and Friedrichstrasse, very close to the sector boundary. After a short consultation with my mother, I was allowed to register. The holiday camps were, for example, in Pätz, Prieros and

Biesenthal, always on some lakes. In 1946 I took part in a holiday camp in Pätz. I liked it very much. The food was completely sufficient and tidy, which was very important for the time. Members of the Soviet Army talked about well-known Russian writers such as Dostoyevsky and Tolstoy. One film sticks in my memory, namely "Children around Ludwig Renn" or something similar, which was filmed in my summer camp in Biesenthal a year later, with a number of children playing along, including myself. In this second summer camp, which I attended again in 1947, it was nice again.

In the second holiday camp, in addition to this film, which was shot, a Red Army officer also gave a lecture about his father, and about his family in general, who should have fled from the National Socialists in Heidelberg. I didn't really understand anything. He often mentioned the Red Army and Heidelberg, and Stuttgart too, he also spoke of his father, who is said to have been a doctor there. It wasn't until much later that his name Wolf told me something, namely as the name of the second man in the GDR State Security Service. Had this man given the lecture?

The holiday camp in Biesenthal came to an end just as it did in Pätz. I liked it again, but slowly the relationship between West Berlin and East Berlin changed. Political relations became unfriendly and changed. In 1948 there was the blockade. With the airlift, the Americans then captured the hearts of the people of West Berlin.

I also consider the story of my grandmother Emilie Giese to be worth mentioning. She was 65 years old at the time, but aged a lot. After this incident, which she often recounted, Russian soldiers apparently saved her life.

My grandmother lived with her husband, my grandfather Wilhelm, in Briesen in West Prussia, a small town about 120 kilometers south of Danzig. When the Soviet Army approached the city and everything fled, my grandfather insisted on staying in Briesen with his wife. When the Red Army took this small town, my grandfather fell ill and had to stay in bed. Shortly afterwards, three young Poles appeared, insulted and insulted Grandfather and strangled him while lying in bed. Grandmother was held and had to watch everything. Then she was able to tear herself away and ran away. Apparently, she was not persecuted.

She reached the barn of a refugee farmer and stayed there for about a day. It was bitterly cold outside. Then she dared to go back to her house. A tenant in her house, who had remained a Pole during the German period, made a coffin in my grandfather's carpentry workshop.

Grandma made the interior out of sheets and they both took the body to the cemetery in a handcart. There they dug a primitive pit with a spade and hoe, because the ground was frozen, and buried my grandfather.

Shortly afterwards, Soviet soldiers showed up and took my grandmother away. They indicated that they would be placed in a kind of "protective camp" to be protected from the revenge of the Poles. Briesen had become Polish again. Indeed it was. In this camp there were a large number of mainly older Germans who were simply but adequately fed and had a place to sleep, but also had to work. In short, they were protected. They shouldn't leave the camp. After two years, grandmother was sent to the East Zone by train and came to Berlin. Since our address had not changed, she found us and stayed with us for a while.

I described this episode to point out the possible Soviet protective camp. Except from my grandmother, I have never heard of such institutions. This camp, or whatever Grandma thought it was, must have been either south of Danzig, in the area of Graudenz, Briesen or Thorn. But it could also have been further away. My grandmother was never able to say where this protective camp was actually located, but she always mentioned it. My grandmother soon moved from Berlin to our aunt, her other daughter, in Oldenburg. The cities of Graudenz, Thorn and Briesen, in the vicinity of which the camp might have been, are now called Grudziadz, Torun and Wabrzezno.

Lothar Hans Schreiber:

Dr. jur. Dr.med. Lothar Hans Schreiber
lives in St. Wendel in Saarland
(Germany). He grew up in West Berlin
and studied law. As a fully qualified
lawyer, he was given the opportunity to
complete a medical degree with the
Bundeswehr. He is a government
director a. D. and Chief Medical Officer
d. R. and has given lectures as a lecturer

at 2 technical universities in the field of addiction medicine, as well as published numerous scientific papers. In addition to his professional duties, he dealt intensively with recent history, in particular with events at the end of the war and the post-war period. He is married, has two grown sons and 3 grandchildren who live abroad.

St. Wendel

Germany

2021